YOU CAN'T HAVE SUNBEAMS WITHOUT LITTLE SPECKS OF DUST

Household hints, Quotes and Anecdotes

By Barbara Shook Hazen

The C. R. Gibson Company
Norwalk, Connecticut

"For every evil under the sun,
There is a remedy, or there is none.
If there be one, try and find it;
If there be none, never mind it."

Old Nursery Rhyme

INTRODUCTION

Here is the perfect (and perfectly amusing) answer to the harried houseperson's* plea for HELP!

* * In cooking, cleaning, and making the most of your time, money and storage space.

* * In coping with ink stains (use milk) and polishing silver when you've just run out of silver polish (use toothpaste instead).

* * In conserving energy, cut flowers and your sense of humor.

* * Even in cleaning your glasses (try a dollar bill and see).

Presented in this one eye-catching collection are invaluable hints, shortcuts, and gems of wisdom to make your day smoother and your load lighter. Plus quotes and tidbits to tickle your funnybone and put a smile under your thinking cap.

* regardless of age, sex or housekeeping style

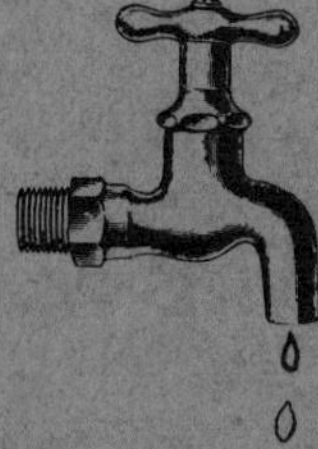

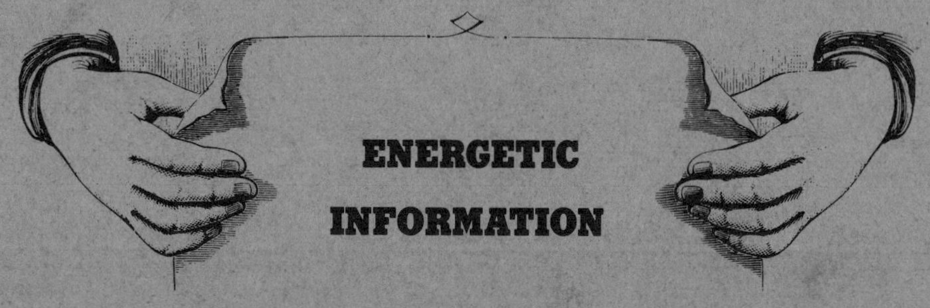

A black and white TV set uses a third less energy than color. Also, most sets use electricity even when not in use. Always unplug before you go away.

Water wise. Turn single-lever faucets back to cold. Hot water takes energy.

Light wise. Use long-life bulbs only in high or inaccessible places, as they use more energy.

Keep the heat. Dry consecutive loads of laundry.

When cooking, keep a closed-door policy.
Peeking prolongs time, wastes energy.

Perk up personal energy with a jump rope, jog
around the block, quick cat nap.

Save Energy, Save $$$

A laundry hang-up is good for you. Great
exercise, save $ and energy — and you can chat
with the neighbors.

And did you know that it takes twice as much
energy to dry a load of laundry as it takes to wash
it!

Walk — anywhere under 10 blocks.

Turn the furnace down — a cool head thinks clearer.

Dine by candlelight.

The Second Time Around

Trimmed greeting cards make nifty gift tags.
Punch a hole in one corner of the design and
draw through colored string or ribbon.

Re-use gift ribbons ironed out with a hair curling
iron.

Follow, follow, follow
tag sale signs
and second-hand ads in the local Penny Saver.
Support church and charity bazaars.

Second hand shopping is more fun to do than buying brand new.

New Tricks for Old Nylon Stockings

Use them to
 1) Store plant bulbs in the feet. Hang high and
    dry.
 2) Stash camphor balls in and put in your silver
    chest. (Keeps silver from oxidizing.)
 3) Stuff with mothballs and hang in back of the
    closet.
 4) Cover a bristly hairbrush with for a quick,
    dry shampoo.
 5) Line wool sleeves if you're allergic.
 6) Stuff saggy upholstery and pillows.

7) Stuff an old hot-water bottle to use as a
   kneeling pad.
8) Strain fat.
9) Use instead of string for tying bundles really
   tightly.
10) Wrap wire coat hangers to keep clothes from
    slipping.
11) Make a scary Hallowe'en mask.
12) Stuff a toe with catnip to make a cat happy.

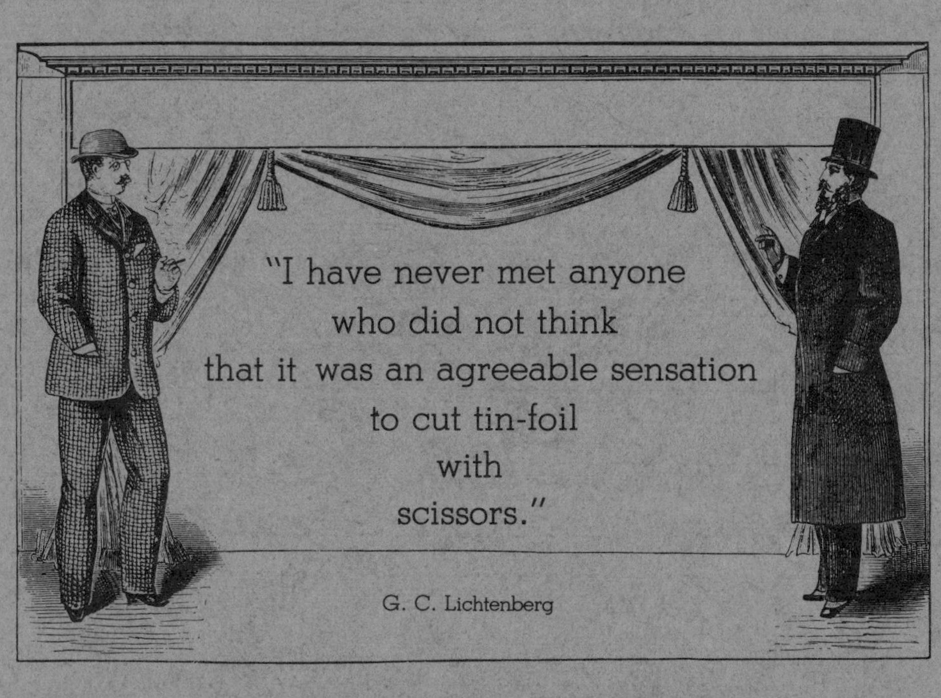

"I have never met anyone
who did not think
that it was an agreeable sensation
to cut tin-foil
with
scissors."

G. C. Lichtenberg

Foiled Again (or Other Uses For Tinfoil)

Use foil frozen-food pans for mixing paint and messy household jobs. Tossing away saves cleaning up.

Put foil pans under flowerpots.

Use aluminum foil to mend a scratched mirror. Smooth over the back of the mirror; then coat with shellac.

Cover children's schoolbooks with foil.

Make table pads by wrapping foil around shirt cardboards.

Line the bottom of your bird cage with tinfoil — *if* you have a bird.

Re-Use, Re-Cycle

Egg cartons make great

    jewelry cases
    nail and toolbox trays
    spring bulb keepers
    office supply stashes (paper clips, rubber
        bands, etc.)
    stamp sorters

Befriend a bird. Save the lint from the dryer filter.
In spring, put out of doors so the birds can use it
as nesting material.

Recycle tin cans into colorful pencil holders.
Cover with bright adhesive paper.

"An egg is always an adventure."

Oscar Wilde

"We can lick gravity, but sometimes the
paperwork is overwhelming."

Wernher Von Braun

Modern Day Dilemma:
Paper, paper, everywhere
and not enough time to think.

Solution: Handle each piece of paper (bill or
letter or memo) only once.
Answer, file or dispose of.

Grade Paperwork and Tasks

A = Essential. Do at once!
B = Important. But can be put off a bit.
C = Can be put off indefinitely. But not forever.
D = Deep-six in the wastebasket. NOW!

Keep A's and B's in separate file boxes. Stash C's
in a grocery carton, which you go over monthly.
You'll find the C's have a way of sorting
themselves out.

NOTE: It is a good idea to keep a separate file for
all financial or money-related matters.

Memo To: The Future
From: Me

1) Write down 5 long term goals—where do I
   really want to be in 5 years and what do I want
   to be doing?
2) Write down ONE thing I can do concretely
   NOW toward getting there.
3) Take one small step—TODAY!

If you can't figure out what you really want, have
a one-person brainstorming session.
    1) Take a large piece of lined paper.
    2) Writing fast and free, list things you *like* to
       do.
    3) On a 2nd piece of paper, list what you *are*
       doing.
    4) Compare and consider.

memo

File Tips
Cluster information under the *largest possible*
category — car, house, kids, taxes, etc.

Keep a file marked "hangover" for nasty old
business. Tackle on days you're feeling brave —
Or
    Whittle it away
    An item a day.

Keep in mind that more people are defeated by
overcomplex systems than by not filing at all!

There are only two kinds of things to do:
Those you have to, and those you want to.

There are two categories of people to see:
Those you have to, and those you want to.

Remembering this helps set priorities and
eliminates a lot of in-between.

File A to Z
to find it easily.

"Your ship can't come in until you straighten out
your port."

Gwen Davis

Organization Plus

Tackle impossible clutter piecemeal — one drawer, one shelf, one section.

Don't let a day go by without doing at least one segment.

Keep a running "To-Do" List. Cross off each accomplishment with a bright felt-tip pen.

Keep a "Hem 'N Haw" box for "can't decides."

Nothing is more time consuming —

exhausting — than indecision.

Resolved

To keep a household loose-leaf notebook.
In it, keep a room by room inventory.
Have a page for each closet, a special page for
winter-summer storage.
Write in pencil and date each item.

(A good place for all your vital household
information — workmen, warranties, subscriptions,
etc., etc.)

"The first great rule of life is to put up with
things."
Baltasar Gracián

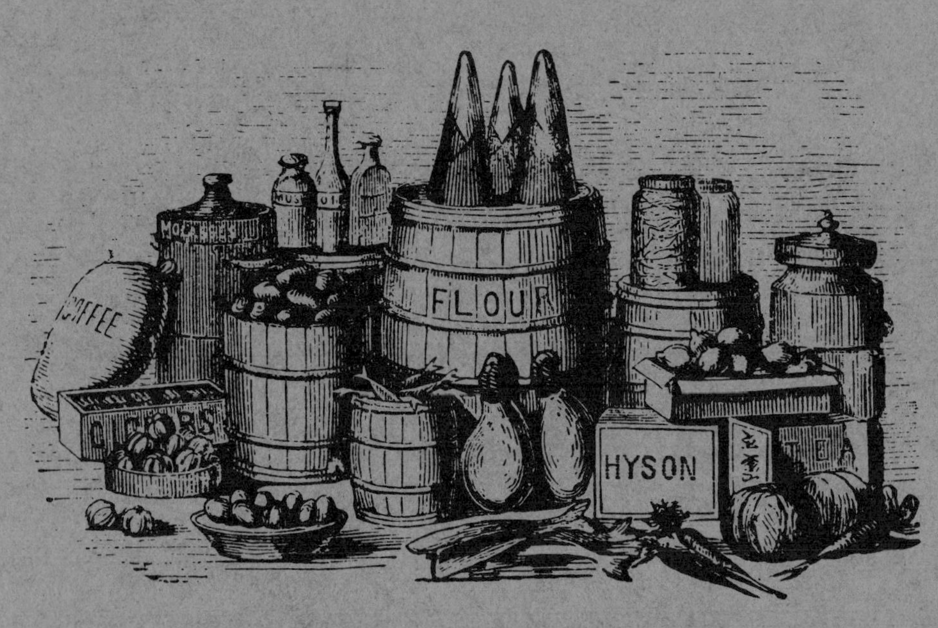

MOLASSES
COFFEE
MUSTARD
FLOUR
HYSON
TEA

Resolved

To use up all older canned goods before they lose their vitamins. And toss out the real oldies.

To get rid of all dribs and drabs in the cleaning supply cabinet.

To set up a mini-toolchest just for me. So I'll always have a hammer, wrench and screwdriver handy.

To throw it out if I don't know what it's for. (And not complain if I find out later.)

To deep-six spices that have turned to straw. Or any over a year old.

"Nothing puzzles me more than time and space;
and yet nothing puzzles me less, for I never think
about them."

Charles Lamb

The main difference between time and money
is that you can pile up pennies
in an old applesauce jar
but you can't hold over
even a second of today till tomorrow.

Segal's Law
A man with one watch knows what time it is.
A man with two watches is never sure.

Tip: Make prime use of your time and space.
Keep small dust-catching collections in glass
cases.

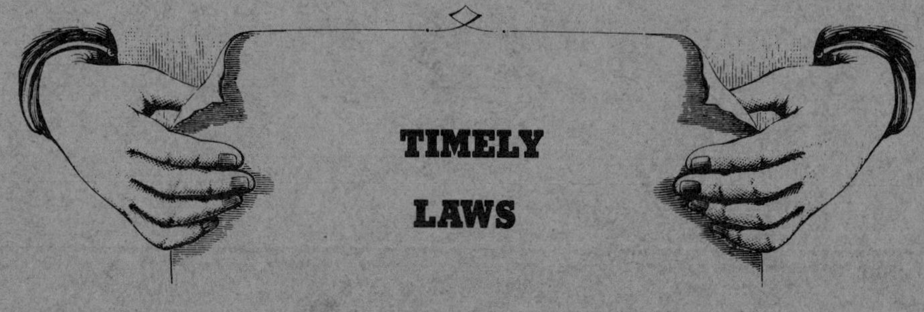

Always carry something with you to read, write on or mull over. If you have to wait — at airports, stations, doctors' offices, etc. — you won't be wasting time.

Ninety-Ninety Rule of Project Schedules
The first 90% of the task takes 90% of the time, and the last 10% takes the other 90%.

"Everything comes to him who hustles while he waits."

Thomas Edison

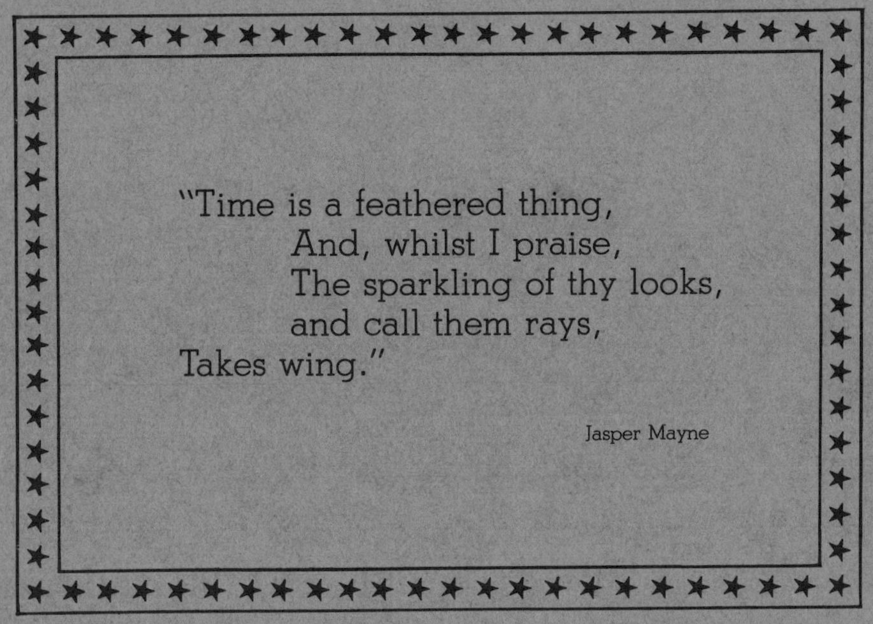
"Time is a feathered thing,
And, whilst I praise,
The sparkling of thy looks,
and call them rays,
Takes wing."

Jasper Mayne

Save Time, Save Steps

Tuck a dustcloth in every room.

In every bathroom keep a sponge, a small container of scouring powder, and an old toothbrush to clean tile and grout.

Hose down porches and patios instead of sweeping.

Put a long cord on the telephone so you can do something else while you're talking on it.

"The Man with a new idea is a Crank until the idea succeeds."

Mark Twain

"Cocks crow in the morn
        To tell us to rise,
And he who lies late
        Will never be wise;
For early to bed
        And early to rise
Is the way to be healthy,
        And wealthy, and wise."

Old Nursery Rhyme

"Everybody talks about water pollution, but no
one seems to know who started it."

Art Buchwald

"It is well to put off until tomorrow what you
ought not to do at all."

Author Unknown

Never clean above the eye level of the tallest
person who comes to visit.

But setting the timer for "just five minutes" is an invaluable aid to getting into a difficult or resistance-producing task. Once started, you're likely to keep on going.

Reward yourself once you have polished off the
sticky wicket. Read a book, take a swim, go smell
the flowers. This is called "positive reinforcement"
and may propel you to go on to more difficult
tasks.

"Our life is frittered away by detail . . . .
Simplify, simplify."

Henry David Thoreau

"Time is a circus always packing up
and moving away."

Ben Hecht

"Unless hours were cups of sack, and minutes
capons . . . and the blessed sun himself a fair
wench in flame-color'd taffeta, I see no reason
why thou shouldst be so superfluous to demand
the time of the day."

William Shakespeare

Getting up *one* hour earlier will add years to your
life and give you time to jog, read,
or work on a pet project while the house is quiet.

"Time is something we ain't got nothing but."

American saying

"You may delay, but time will not."

Benjamin Franklin

"Now's the day and now's the hour."

Robert Burns

Timely Tips

"Time is a dressmaker specializing in alterations."

Faith Baldwin

Jump rope for 10 minutes a day, lose 10 pounds in
a year.

Write a page a day, have a 365 page book at the
end of the year.

Write a letter a week, you'll have kept up with 52
friends.

"The most instructive experiences are those of
everyday life."

Frederich Nietzsche

Serve simple meals on your prettiest plates.

Serve diet dinners on salad or luncheon plates.

Spices add variety to life

Try nutmeg on spinach.

Parsley, fennel and cloves make fine breath
fresheners.

Add a pinch of:
      thyme to carrots
      mint to peas
      basil to tomatoes
      dill to potatoes
      sage to chicken
      oregano to eggs

"Small cheer and great welcome makes a merry
feast."

William Shakespeare

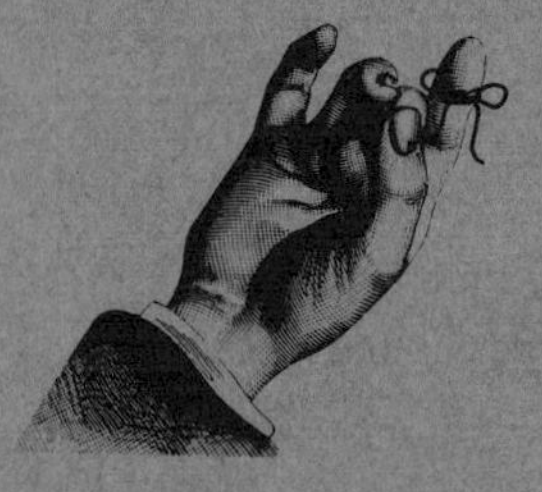

(Because one thing you can usually count on remembering is that you won't.)

Label rarely-used keys with colored cardboard discs. Keep in one drawer or pot.

Keep cords in seldom-used appliances. Or, pin a note to the electric blanket telling where you put the cord.

Keep a roll of packing tape by the fridge. Date and label as you stash.

Also . . .

Keep a communal bulletin board near the telephone.

Keep paper, push pins and a permanently attached pencil within arm's reach.

A letter-embossing tape labeler is an organized person's best friend.

Use it to mark tools, drawers, spice canisters, medicines, cabinets, shelves. The labels are clear, yet come off easily.

"In living with less clutter in a life, the mind also becomes less cluttered."

Dorothy Gilman

Some are wise, and some are otherwise.

Proverb

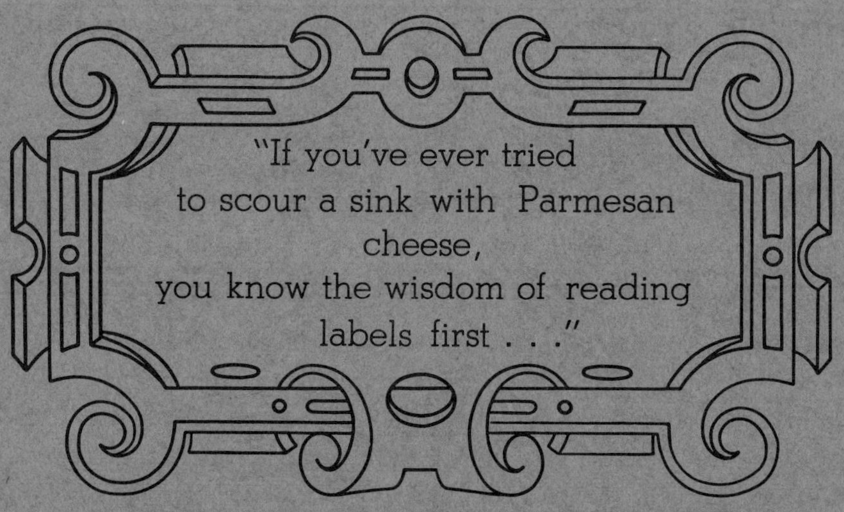

Dereck Williamson

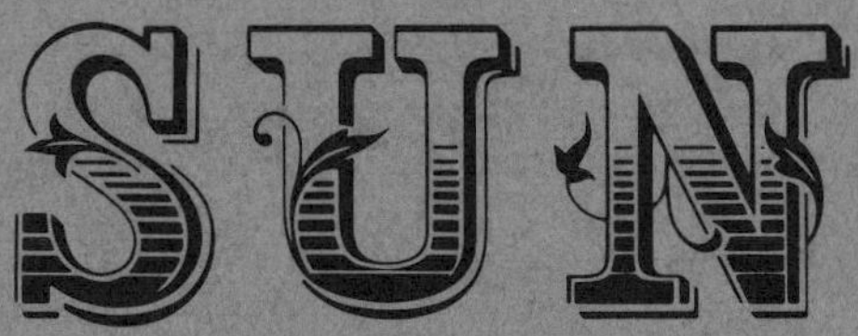

Imperfect Words to Live By

A half-baked job is better than nothing done at all.

Perfection is the pits.

Who *wants* to eat off the floor.

Spotless isn't very interesting.

BEAM

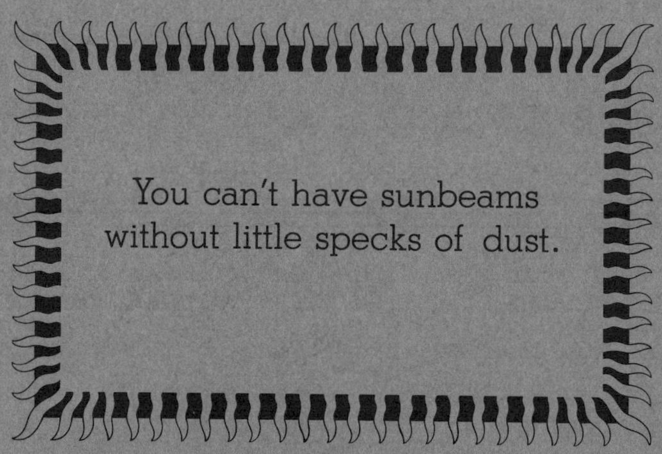

You can't have sunbeams
without little specks of dust.

All except very hairy plants love to be misted as well as watered.

Put pebbles in pot bottoms for better drainage.

Re-pot at the end of the resting season (usually late winter).

To Make Cut Flowers Last Longer

Gather in the cool of the evening (or early morning).

Keep in cool water if you can't arrange right away.

Strip the stems of foliage that will be under water.

Use sharp cutting tools.

Always cut on the slant.

Going away but don't have anyone to water?

Don't despair. Do cut lengths of cotton cord
(shoelaces will do) long enough to reach from a
glass tumbler bottom to 1½" in the plant soil.
Fill and wave bye-bye.

water your plants, set in the tub on a
newspaper bed and cover lightly with plastic.

RX for Special Flower Friends

Asters & Marigolds: Add sugar and salt to water.

Carnations: Cool water.

Daisies: Add a half dozen drops of peppermint oil.

Day Lily and Funkia: A quarter cup vinegar to 1 cup cold water.

Lilac: Leave on the green leaves near the flower head.

Petunia: Add a little sugar.

Tulip: Use COLD water. Roll in wet paper to straighten stems.

Violets: Put UNDER water for an hour after picking. Then place in ICE water.

A posy in your lapel
proclaims your world is well.

"I never met a house plant

I didn't like."

Jerry Baker

Re: Watering Plants

Bring water to room temperature. Let sit to get rid of chlorine.

Always water bulbs from the bottom.

Stale club soda has trace minerals that are good for plants. Ditto, cooled boiled-egg water.

Overwatering kills more plants than any disease. If the soil feels moist, wait.

Green-Thumb Tip: Snow is good for green and growing plants — has needed nutrients and minerals.

"Snow is faked cleanliness."

Goethe

Presto. Change the color of your cut flowers overnight by putting the stems in a solution of warm water and food coloring.

Your houseplants will like you better if you hum to them, inquire about their health, and wash their leaves* once a month with very mild soap and water.

*Exception: hairy plant friends.

In winter, force flowering shrubs by putting paper
towels soaked in ammonia around the container
you put them in. The fumes do the trick.

Clean artificial flowers by shaking in a bag with
salt.

Revive real flowers by plopping briefly in very
hot water.

Clean leaves with glycerine or a milk and water
solution.

Make pots perkier with contact paper.

Give milk to growing tomatoes.

Make your own plant food: Mush vegetable peelings and parings in the electric blender.

Make your own insect spray of crushed pepper and garlic plus water.

A birdcage makes a good home
for a trailing plant.

Give droopy ferns
— and other green plants —
a cold cup of tea.

CAR NOTES

Put gravel, sand or baking soda in the bottom of your car's ash tray so cigarettes don't smoulder.

Prevent doors from freezing shut in winter by wiping the rubber gaskets with vegetable oil.

A ball of tinfoil will remove rust from your bumper.

Save Gas

Up to 10% when you buy radial tires.
Up to 15% for a well-tuned car.
Up to 30% for driving at 50 m.p.h. on long trips,
rather than speeding.
Up to 100% for biking instead. Or walking.

Invaluable Auto Accessories

Clip-on tissue box.

Conveniently tied trash bag.

Working flashlight — for map readings and emergencies.

Magnetic coin holder — for tolls, bridges.

A friend with a good sense of direction.

Stash a half dozen composition shingles in the trunk. Easier to carry than sand, just as effective when you are stuck.

A shoe bag makes a good car tote.

For safety's sake: carry flares.

The more you do, the easier it becomes.

Develop your own style. You don't have to entertain in kind, just your kind of way.

Mix 'n match — plates, kinds of people, couples and singles.

Expect some surprises.

Keep a special party shelf for uninvited guests.
Stock with tinned pâté, smoked oysters, other
delicacies. As well as melba rounds, paper
napkins, etc.

Make double-order party dishes. One for now,
one to freeze for next time.

Repeat to yourself: "The world won't end if
everything isn't done before they come."
(Some of the best parties begin in the kitchen.)

And, "There is no such animal as a perfect
host/hostess."

Need an extra hand?
Borrow a neighbor's child — frequently more
efficient than one of your own.
Kids can tote coats, pass trays, answer bells —
and free you to do more complex tasks.

Invariable Rule

When the place is a mess,
expect the unexpected guest.

When it happens,
don't hide or apologize,
do grab your coat, close the door
and go OUT for coffee.
Often an old friend is best enjoyed
in a fresh scene.

Unnatural Laws of Entertaining

If there is less than a 1% chance it will rain the day of the picnic, party, wedding, or whatever, it will.

If there is one dish your guest of honor is allergic to, it will be the one you cooked especially for him/her.

If there is one guest who lingers,
it will be your least favorite.

"The golden rule
is that there are no golden rules."

George Bernard Shaw

Keep a list in the back of your calendar of people you owe and/or want to have over.

Keep a guest book. Get all your guests to sign. Fun now. More fun later.

A real friend is someone who helps you out even when she isn't invited.
(Like feeding your kids when your boss comes to dinner.)

After a really big party, plan to eat out, have a
soothing massage or go to the movies — AFTER
cleaning up.

Tip: Save the surfaces of valuable tables.
Cover with felt.
(Red for Christmas parties.)
Saves work, too.

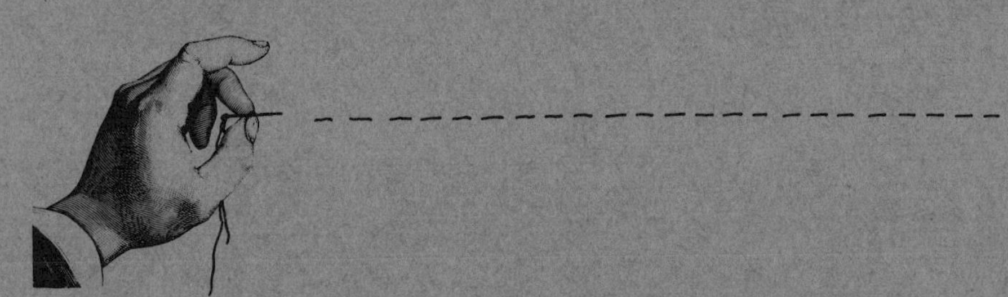

SEW-SEW IDEAS

As you sew, so shall you keep your coat buttoned.

A bar of soap makes a perfect pin cushion and the pins slide through material more easily.

Zippers zip zippier when rubbed with soap or wax paper.

"Antique" white thread by dipping it in tea.

Pre-shrink cotton thread by dropping the spool in hot water. Dry before using. This avoids puckered seams.

Use an empty matchbook as a sample case for yarn. Tape, wind, close. Keeps it clean, too.

Wind embroidery thread on plastic hair curlers.

Use corrugated cardboard as a knitting-needle case.

Need someone to hold your knitting yarn? Find a lampshade the right size.

Oiled cracker-box papers make good rustproof needle cases.

Having trouble pushing the needle through your sewing material? Run the needle through your hair — *very* carefully.

A needle is easier to thread if you cut the thread
on the diagonal and work over white paper.

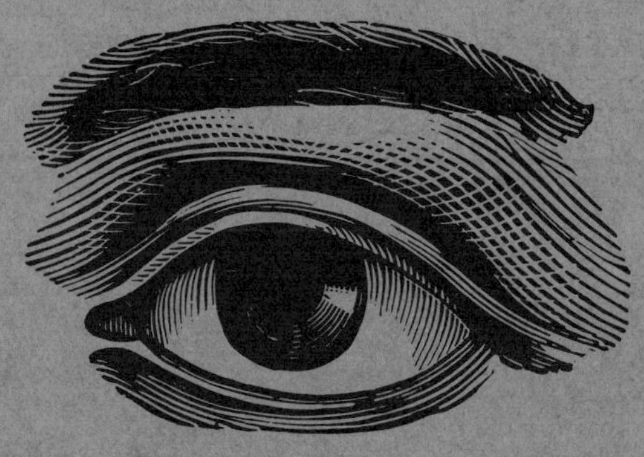

Getting The Thread Through the Eye
of the Needle

Stiffen with hair spray.

Or colorless nail polish.

Or prick your finger, turn into a princess and
give up sewing for ever after.

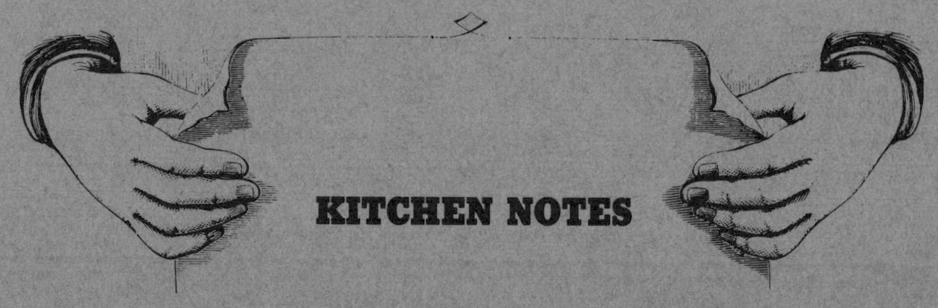

KITCHEN NOTES

Store your flashlight in the refrigerator to make batteries last longer. And, in an emergency, you'll know where one is.

Pears ripen faster if you put an apple in the same bag.

Pick out a stray piece of eggshell easily by scooping it out with the empty shell half. It really works!

Does soap powder make you sneeze? It won't if you put a teaspoon of salt in the soap box.

Handy Food Bits

Dress cucumbers deliciously with cole slaw dressing.

Wrap ears of corn in tinfoil and grill for a tasty change. (Grilled eggplant is a treat, also any "meaty" vegetable.)

Good use for sour milk — soak silverware in it, to make it shine.

Before you pitch moldy cheese, cover it in a container with a few sugar lumps. Wait, and watch the mold disappear like magic.

Don't throw in the sour sponge, soak in salt water or baking soda.

Revive stale shelled nuts by placing in a flat
tinfoil pan and putting in a 300° oven for 10
minutes.

Candy pies are dandy. Use the crust left over
from the big pie, then just dot generously with
butter and brown sugar.

To Cut Food Bills

Buy seasonal specials,

Buy in bulk,

Make more vegetable  egg main dishes.

Serve slightly smaller portions. (It has been scientifically proven that most adult Americans eat too much.)

Go visiting.

Go on a diet NOW.

"Nothing helps scenery like ham and eggs."

Mark Twain

Set the basic breakfast table *before* you go to bed. Finding something done first thing in the morning is like getting an unexpected check.

Neat Tricks with Peanut Butter

Use it to clean chrome,
remove chewing gum from a child's skin,
and take off the sticky glue residue
after pulling off an adhesive price tag.

Better yet — make a peanut-butter ball and give it
to the birds.

Still better yet — mix liberally with marshmallow
fluff (or bananas or strawberry jam) and give the
kids a treat.

(Or mix with chutney to make a sophisticated
cocktail spread.)

Not-So-Sour Notes

When you're stuck with lemons, make lemonade.

A lemon is only an orange with an inferiority complex.

"I'll be with you in the squeezing of a lemon."

Oliver Goldsmith

Longer Mileage Out of Your Lemons

Refrigerate your lemons (also parsley & watercress) in an airtight glass container. An applesauce jar is ideal.

To release more juice, roll on the counter top before using.

When you want just a little juice, spear with a knitting needle or ice pick. Squeeze, then seal with adhesive tape.

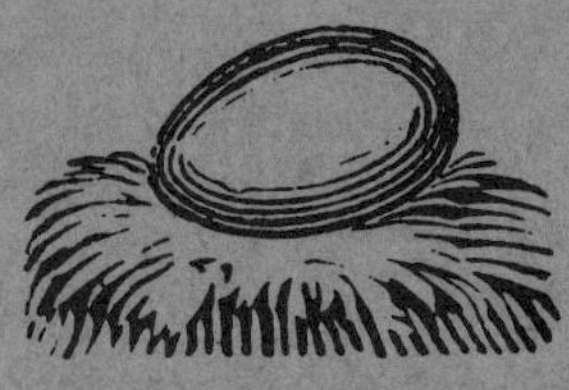

Eggs-pert Advice

A pinch of flour sprinkled into hot fat will prevent frying eggs from popping.

"Beat" eggs by shaking them vigorously in a glass jar. (Saves dishwashing, too.)

For unbroken yolks, break the *whole* egg into your bowl. Then, with a *tablespoon,* go under the yolk and lift it out.

Light Sayings

It is better to light one candle than curse the utility company.

Candlelight is the perfect cover-up for housekeeping sins of omission.

> "Jack, be nimble,
> Jack, be quick,
> Jack, jump over the candlestick."

Candle Tips

Candles soaked in salt water will drip less.

Candles kept in the refrigerator 24 hours before
using will burn more evenly.

To get candle wax off metal candlesticks, put them
in the freezer.

To get candle wax off your carpet, cover the spot
with a brown paper bag. Iron the bag, which acts
as a blotter, with a warm iron.

A clothesline waxed with candle wax will last
longer.

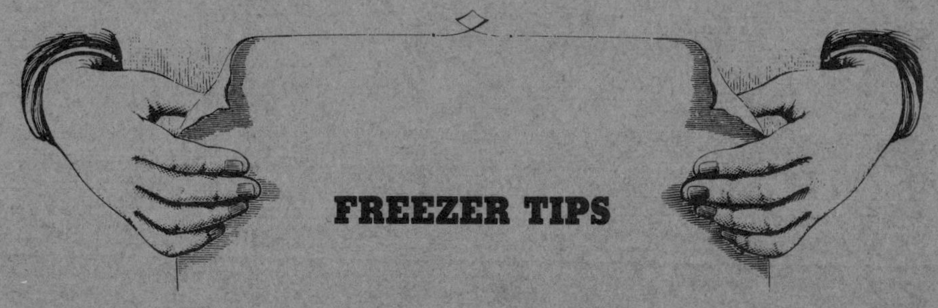

FREEZER TIPS

Freeze a little before you freeze a lot.

Don't freeze anything with mayonnaise in it.

Double wrapping helps prevent freezer burn.

Always have an understudy dish in case what you counted on unfreezes funny.

Keep in mind that some flavors like onion, salt
and chili pepper tend to tame in the freezer.
Others, like garlic, get stronger, and potatoes,
carrots, squash and beans tend to get mushy.
TASTE before you serve up.

Memo to Me

Avoid unnecessary freezer openings. Note what's
inside — and when it went in. Attach note to
fridge with fun magnetic holder. Scratch off the
old, add on the new.

Combine a frozen main dish with a garden fresh
salad. Not a frozen vegetable.

Rejuvenate an ailing frozen dish with fresh
ingredients — peppers, mushrooms, dillweed, etc.
If dry, add boullion, tomato juice or milk.

Your Favorite Color Around the House and What It Says About You

Yellow — You're optimistic, have a sunny outlook on life.

Blue — You're poised, somewhat conservative, occasionally moody.

Green — You are relaxed, gregarious, and a nature lover.

Red — You're lively, extroverted, liking fast cars
    and fast music.

Orange — You're up-to-date, youthful in outlook,
    and somewhat of a gourmet.

Neutral Colors (Off-whites, beige and gray) —
    Far from being colorless, yours is a
    well-knit, well-rounded personality. Your
    color preference is an ideal background
    for your integrated tastes and varied
    friends.

MISCELLANEOUS MAGIC

A wallet or coin purse with a rubber band around it won't slip out of your pocket.

Rub tar off your skin with the outside of an orange peel.

Rub fruit stains off with corn meal and vinegar.

Remove fuzz balls from sweaters by shaving — *gently* — with an electric razor.

Quick-dry nail polish by putting your hands in the freezer. Count to 10.

Clean silver jewelry by dunking in a quarter cup
baking soda plus a tablespoon water.

To help prevent tarnish, put a piece of chalk in
your jewelry box.

Take the sting out of insect bites with cider
vinegar. Or baking soda. Or meat tenderizer.

Dirty eyeglasses and no water anywhere? Clean
them in a jiffy with a dollar bill. (Any
denomination will do.)
(When you do wash them, add a drop of vinegar.
They'll dry streakless.)

Rubbing alcohol will prevent razor-blade rust.

A sponge in the umbrella stand will get rid of
drips.

For really soft hair, rinse in rain water.

"Don't put up your umbrella until it begins to rain."

Lord Samuel

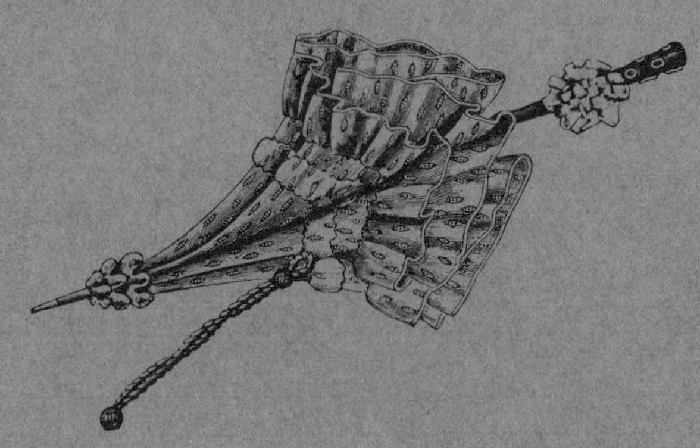

Spice up your winter woolies

Put cloves in coat pockets. Keeps moths away and smells nice.

Put blue tissue paper around valuable papers — and linens — keeps them from yellowing.

Travel Flash

Need a change of scene but don't want to spend a bundle?
Trade houses (or apartments) over the holidays or for a month in the summer. Communicate through the classifieds or an agency specializing in house swaps.

There's nothing like getting away to get you back in gear.

Friends and Neighbors

Organize a neighborhood exercise class. Rotate houses.

Have a yearly block party.

Set up a toy swap.
Or
kids' clothing exchange.
Or
mini lending library.

It takes two
to make doing dishes fun.

Form a baby sitting co-op.

Take turns cooking for each other's parties — or
just for the fun of it.

Trade services — like plant watering, weeding,
walking the dog, etc. Do for your neighbor what
you do best. And vice versa.

Do small pesky tasks (like sewing) communally —
and companionably — over coffee.

United you save. Buy firewood, meat, etc. in
bulk.

Buy "shares" in major items like power
lawn mowers, roto-tillers.

"After the verb 'To Love,' 'To Help' is the most
beautiful verb in the world."

Baroness von Stuttner

Refrigerator Notes

An open box of baking soda will chase food smells away. Replace after several months.

Vanilla on a cotton ball will also make your fridge smell sweet.

Best bet refrigerator cleaner: Baking soda & water.

Deter refrigerator raiders by marking "forbidden" items with masking tape or a red pencil — like the cookies for the bake sale and the pâté for tomorrow's party.

Psychological Note

You can tell a lot about a person by a quick glance at the contents of his or her refrigerator. Whether the person is messy or neat, slapdash or orderly, spendthrift or frugal, a "keeper" or a "tosser," a morning or evening type, creative or conservative.

Memo to me
Re: Fry Pans

Food won't stick if I heat the pan BEFORE adding the butter or oil.

Remind myself that a little salt prevents a lot of spatter.

Tip for the Working Houseperson

Post dinner menus and recipes in a set place on bulletin board or fridge. Hopefully, if you're late, some other family member will start the meal moving.

To The Rescue!

De-grease gravy with baking soda.

Revive wilted lettuce by dousing first in hot water, then ice water with a teaspoon of lemon juice or vinegar.

When cream won't whip, add egg white. OR whip in a little bowl over a bigger bowl of ice cubes.

Soften hardened brown sugar (or marshmallows)
by putting fresh bread in the same box. Re-seal as
tightly as possible.

To take the fat off the top of the stew pot, drop in
lettuce leaves or ice cubes, which the fat will cling
to. (Even easier, refrigerate overnight. The fat will
solidify.)

Kitchens aren't just for cooking.
Make yours a real creative center
for desk work
and fix-it work
and entertaining
and your pet project or hobby —
from pottery to potting petunias.

A bird feeder outside the kitchen window will
provide a never ending nature show.

A kitchen is the ideal place for a small fish tank.
Or shelf garden.

KID STUFF

Clean a beloved stuffed toy by shaking in a bag with corn starch.

Coat precious small fry art work with hair spray.

A lollipop makes a good tongue depressor.

Whisper into the ear of a child who is hurt or angry and crying. He'll stop crying to hear. Then you can calm him down and hug him.

When children's clothing gets a spot, 10 to 1 it's chocolate!

To remove chocolate from washables,
rub the stain in shortening.
Then wash in warm water.

Vegetable bins make great toy stashes because everything is visible.

Feed a sick child on a muffin-tin tray. Almost as much fun as T. W. A.

Kid Trick:
Teach small children to remember their phone
numbers. Match the numbers to the syllables of
their favorite *7-syllable* nursery song.
   Example: 7-6-4-3-2-2-1 instead of Mer-ri-ly we
roll a-long. Or Twin-kle twin-kle lit-tle star.

Dispose of any article of clothing you
        a) haven't worn in a year
        b) can't get into by over two inches
        c) never felt good in
        d) know isn't good enough to give to the
        Smithsonian.

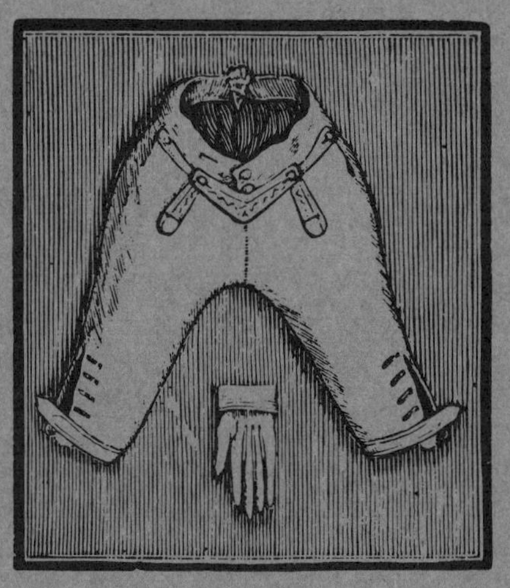

Bundle old clothing off to your local thrift shop
or favorite charity and get a nice fat tax deduction.

Have a mental tag sale. Get rid of any thoughts that are out-dated, worn-out and don't work for you.

Have a real tag sale. Ditto with things.

Less *is* more.
And a lot easier to keep clean.

(On the other hand,
somebody else's treasure
is sometimes your trash
that you tossed out just
before it became valuable —

like political buttons
and first issues of magazines
and unusual liquor or perfume bottles
and hand-crafted items —
all of which tend to increase in value.)

"There are many things that we would throw
away, if we were not afraid that others might pick
them up."

Oscar Wilde

Rule of Thumb for Throwing Away

Give the article the heave-ho
if the answer to both is no.

When in doubt
toss it out.

This above all else I know.
The repairman will come as soon as I go.

If possible, make definite appointments.
If impossible, write a note and make a deal with a
neighbor.

Dishwashing Tips

Avoid the pits. Load silver and stainless in separate compartments.

Fill a badly burned pan immediately with boiling water and baking soda. (Important exception: use COLD water for burnt-on starchy food or milky sauces.)

Rub out tea and coffee stains with baking soda. Or vinegar and salt.

To make glasses sparkle, add ¼ cup white vinegar to the dish water (or dishwasher).

Re: Stainless Steel

Take out spots with white vinegar.

Wipe out streaks with a soft cloth dipped in olive oil.

Make stainless — sinks and tableware — shine by wiping with soda water.

Copper pots can be effectively cleaned with any of these — toothpaste, lemon juice and salt, or catsup.

Or avoid dishes entirely. Have a picnic, indoors or out, or call your favorite pizza parlor or Chinese restaurant with a take-out menu.

TRADE
MIRATUS
STOVE
LONDON
MARK

> "An apple pie without some cheese
> Is like a kiss without a squeeze."
>
>

Keep cheese fresher longer by putting fresh bread in the storage container. Cover tightly with plastic wrap.

Weep no more while peeling onions. Borrow your son's swim goggles.

A lettuce head won't turn brown if you towel wrap it before using.

Use pepper along with other spices. Helps bring out their flavor as well as adding its own.

Natural Wonders

Sip sassafras bark tea in fall,
eat squash-blossom sandwiches in summer*
and *real* snow cones in winter.

*saute lightly in seasoned olive oil.

Re dandelions: Make wine not war —
or
dress the small tender leaves with a vinaigrette
sauce for great salad days.

Put the blossoms in a small glass on the breakfast
table.

Cleanliness is next to Compulsiveness.

To clean grimy telephone dials, wrap facial tissue
around an orange stick or skinny pencil. Dip in
ammonia. Squeeze dry and dial.

To sharpen dull scissors,
cut up sandpaper.

Polish marble with wet chalk.

Clean discolored marble by wiping with
household bleach. Then put in bright sun. Or
under a hot lamp.

Clean glass table tops by wetting with lemon juice
— or ammonia — and drying with the morning
paper.

"Dirt is not dirt, but only matter in the wrong
place."
Lord Palmerston

Polish brass with a paste of lemon juice and salt.

 tomato juice.

 catsup.

"You *always* have options."

Dr. Wayne Dyer

Try toothpaste to take small scratches out of glass.

Mirror, Mirror Fairest of All
Mirrors brighten if a little bluing is added to their
rinse water.

For streakless drying, use your newspaper.

Make cleaning furniture and venetian blinds
easier by putting old soft socks on both hands —
the one to clean with, the other to polish.

"Cleanliness is a fine life preserver."

Clean clear plastic — such as Lucite — with
rubbing alcohol.

Wipe gilt picture frames with beer.
Removes grime without tarnishing.

Clean small-mouthed vases with a mixture of fine
sand, ammonia and water.
Swish, swirl and rinse.

(Note: Colored vases stay cleaner longer. The
color slows down algae growth.)

Perk Up, Pretty Up

Renew rusty scales and medicine cabinets with
bright adhesive paper.

Put gay paper posies — maybe mixed with real
leaves — in dark corners where plants won't
grow.

Note:
Use cologne to wipe yellowed piano keys and turn them white again. (Avoid touching the black keys.)

Clean piano keys with toothpaste.

The Toughest Household Commandment
Envy not those who are naturally neat —
or bake bread
or entertain every week
or make their own slipcovers
or just put in a flagstone terrace
or grew the biggest watermelon on the block.
Think of all the things *you* are neat at doing.

RUN AN
EQUAL OPPORTUNITY
KITCHEN.

EVERYBODY HELPS
EQUALLY.

Unnatural Laws That Can Be Applied To Housework

Murphy's Law
If anything can go wrong, it will.

Law of Selective Gravity
An object will fall so as to do the most damage.

Jenning's Corollary
The chance of the bread falling buttered side down is directly proportional to the cost of the carpet.

*Funny Names for Some Fairly Common Things
You May Have Around the House and Never
Knew What to Call*

AGLET: Metal on shoelace tip, which makes it
    easier to pass through eyelet hole.

QUARREL: Small diamond or square shaped
    pane of glass, as used in lattice windows.

TOBY: Drinking mug shaped like a stout man.

ZARF: Metal holder for coffee cup.

House Blahs Got You Down?

Take a YOU Turn. Consider:
Taking a walk somewhere you've never been.

Calling a friend you haven't seen since high school.

Giving yourself a foot massage.

Planning your next vacation.

Joining a dancing class. (Or exercise)

Taking down the binoculars and going birding.

Beginning a personal diary.

Getting a small fur friend. (Hamsters and gerbils are easy care, even in apartments.)

Breaking routine — go to the movies in
the middle of the day.

Sharing your sinking spell with a good
friend over a hot pot of coffee.

Eating pizza for breakfast.

Buying a good joke book.

Hum while doing
humdrum tasks.

"Things ain't what they used to be and probably never was."

Will Rogers

Tip: If an electric clock starts to buzz turn it upside down and things usually set themselves right.

Key Note
At night, getting into your house is a lark — Just put reflector tape under your keyhole, so you can see it in the dark.

To get rust off your garden tools just fine rub with a soap pad dipped in turpentine.

To prevent loose screws, dip the tip in glue. (Soap to make a screw turn easier.)

When hanging pictures,
drive nails through
crossed pieces of Scotch tape.

The plaster won't
crack.
(And neither will you.)

Dust Detractors

A feather duster.

Fresh flowers. (The eye will always see beauty
before dust balls.)

A cat. (Train him to use his tail.)

Dark glasses.

Good company.

"One keep-clean is better than ten make-cleans."

Author Unknown

Tips for Handling Your Mail

Wet package string before you tie. It stays tauter.

Colorless nail polish over the address will insure that neither snow, sleet nor rain will blotch it up. (For safety's sake, write it on the inside too.)

Pack breakables in popcorn or mini-marshmallows. Tasty bonus for the receiver.

"Presents, I often say, endear absents."

Charles Lamb

There is more than one way to make a bed. Make yours the way you want to lie in it.

In a house with kids — or anyone who hates to make beds — sleeping bags are a great time saver. They avoid nagging, look neat and never come untucked.

RX for Medicine Cabinets

Label all medicines as to purpose, proper dosage and length of time they will remain potent. (Ask when you have the prescription filled.)

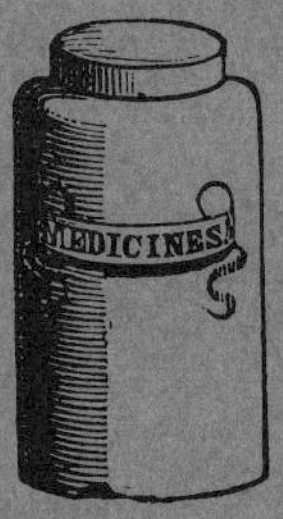

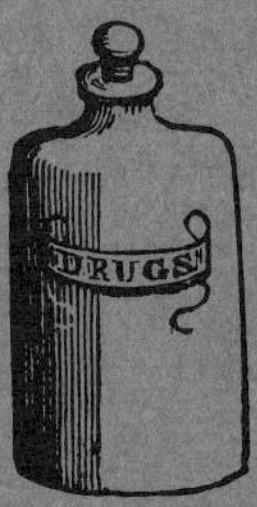

"Laughter is a tranquilizer with no side effects."

Arnold Glasow

Clean out, and clear out once a year.

Empty clear plastic pill containers make ideal-sized travel bottles for shampoo, skin lotion, etc.

Best Bet in the Bathroom

Use baking soda as a
      toothpaste
      mouthwash
      deodorant
      burn remedy
      and all-purpose cleaner.

"Cleanliness is next to elegance."

"What is elegance? Soap and water!"

Tip: Save small soap scraps. Add water to make
your own liquid soap.

For The Time Of Your Life

"He who hesitates is sometimes saved."

James Thurber

When very busy, put off tasks that are neither vitally important nor very interesting. If you close the door, no one need know you didn't make the bed.

"Don't put off for tomorrow what you can do today, because if you enjoy it today, you can do it again tomorrow."

James A. Michener

Do your most important work at YOUR peak time of day. Polish off routine work at other times.

Get as much help as you can (this includes kids).

Don't spend a lot of time doing what you hate and doing it poorly when someone else enjoys it and does it well — anything from carpentry to sewing your own.

Make fast exits from sticky situations.

"A constant smirk upon the face
and a wiffling activity of the body
are strong indications of futility.
*Whoever is in a hurry shows that
the thing he is about is too big for him.*"

Lord Chesterfield

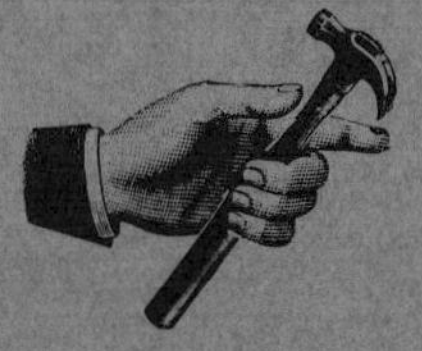

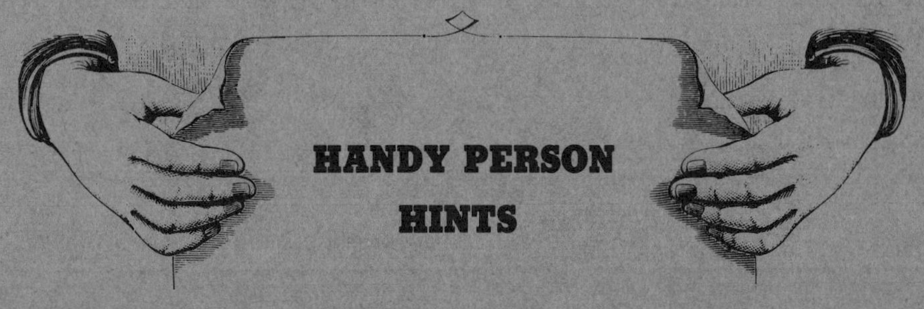

HANDY PERSON HINTS

Remove paint from your hair with warmed white vinegar. It's better to be pickled than painted.

To keep a stepladder from slipping on a wooden floor, slip its feet into your sneakers.

To prevent rust, put several pieces of chalk in your tool box.

A rubber band around a jar lid will make it easier to remove.

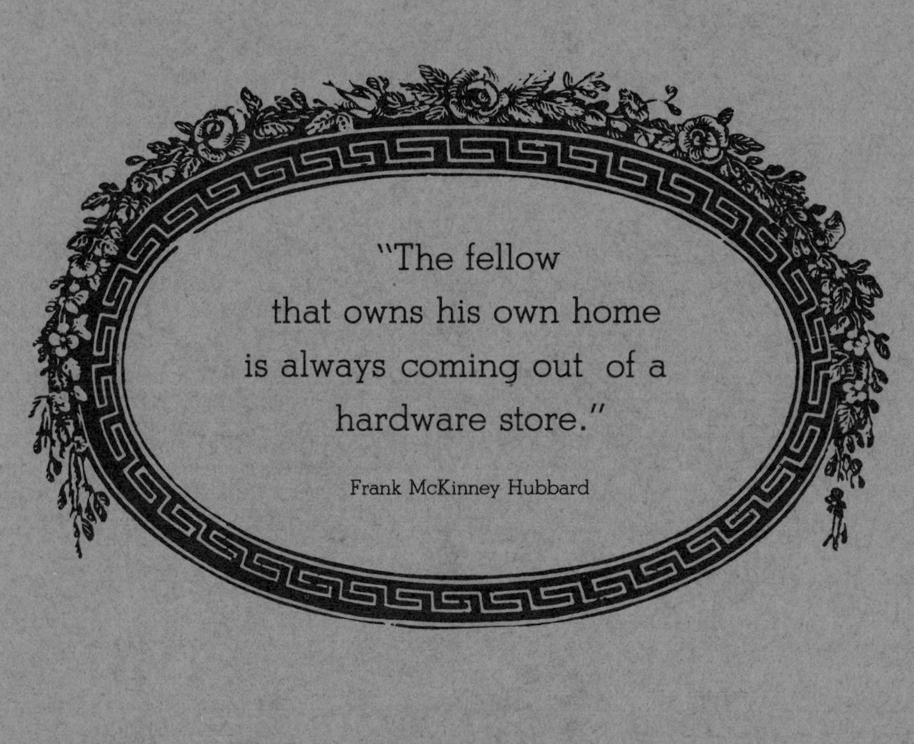
"The fellow
that owns his own home
is always coming out of a
hardware store."

Frank McKinney Hubbard

Rusted nuts and bolts will loosen if you soak them
in soda water.

Sticky drawers will slide better after a wax-paper
rub down.
(A bread wrapper will do nicely.)

Drawer knobs won't wobble if you coat their
screws with clear nail polish.

Winter Wary

Dangerous ice won't form on your front steps if you wash them with hot salty water.

Keep Jack Frost away by rubbing winter windows with a sponge dipped in rubbing alcohol.

For a Cool Summer

Direct your electric fan over a big bowl of ice cubes.

Attach a paper fan to your dog's tail.

Gifty Idea
When you give someone something too big to wrap — like a car, or dishwasher or chair or elephant — send a dime-store replica. Or mount a picture of it on cardboard.

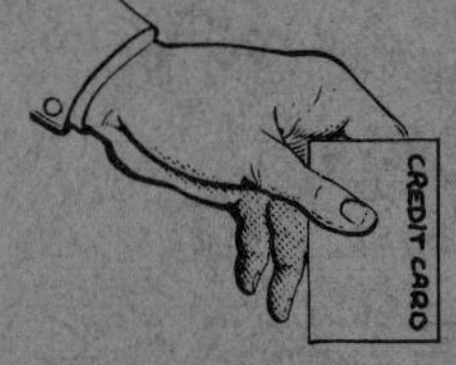

CREDIT CARD

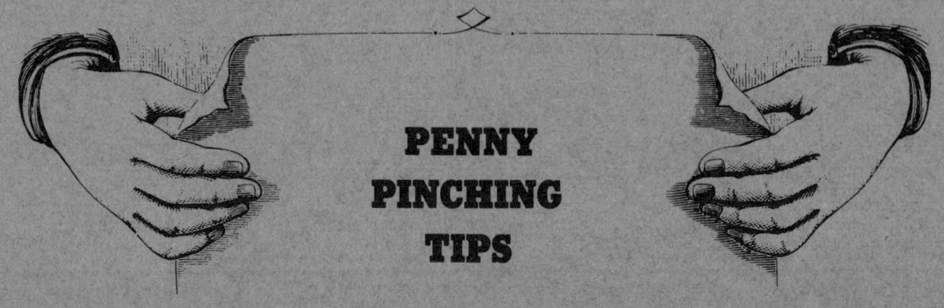

To get the last drop of toothpaste, soak the nearly empty tube in hot water.

Many pennies saved add up to a costly splurge.

Really tight month?
Put yourself on a CASH ONLY basis and hide your credit cards till you catch up.

"It is not a custom with me to keep money to look at."

George Washington

Daily toss small change into a pot, pig or other
saving device. Every few months, exchange for
folding money. Yearly, exchange for a super treat
— like a weekend away. Amazing how it adds up.

Give up smoking
or taxis (walk instead)
or chocolate bars (carrot sticks instead)

Put $5 in the pig bank for each pound you lose.
After each 5 lb. loss, treat yourself to a beautiful
day — at the hairdresser, at the beach —
anything but eating out.

Making It Last Is a Way of Saving

Make bathing caps last longer by dusting with
talcum and storing out-of-season in an air-tight
jar.

Brighten dulled wool rugs by sponging lightly
with warm water plus ½ cup vinegar.

 For easy care
buy wash and wear.

Coat candles used just for decoration with shellac.
They won't get the bends.

Laundry Basket Tips

Really dirty clothes?
Add a little ammonia to the wash water.

Too blue?
Add a little vinegar to the rinse water.

Want white socks? Handkerchiefs?
Boil in lemon water. Or add a pinch of tartar.

Musty bath linen?
Don't throw in the towel. Boil in water plus 3
tablespoons baking soda.

Mildewed clothes?
Moisten with lemon juice. Or buttermilk. Wash,
then dry in the sun.

Make-up marks?
Erase with white bread.

Pantyhose last longer
when lightly starched.
Or frozen before wearing.

Quick — remove that spot!
Shoot the offending stain with shaving cream.

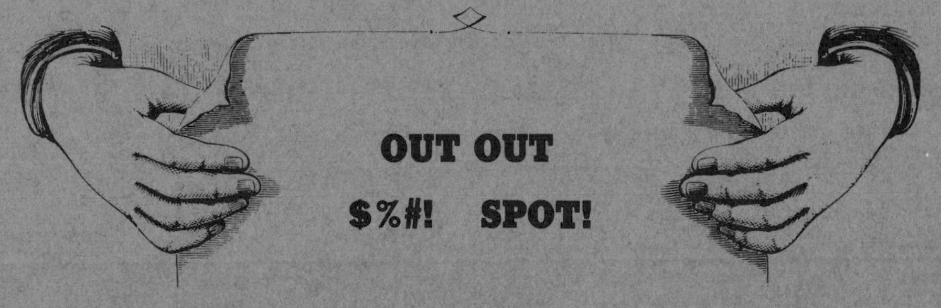

Remove mud spots with raw potato.

Cover a grease spot with flour or talcum. Iron over a plain white blotter.

Use peroxide on scorch spots.

Rub a water ring with a spoon or silver chain.

Fruit Stains

Treat fruit and fruit juice stains as soon as possible. Stretch the stained fabric tightly over a bowl and pour boiling water through the stained area.

Do not use soap.

Do follow up with bleach for white and colorfast fabrics, a white vinegar rinse for others.

Sweaters will wash fluffier if you put a half cup of hair cream rinse in the final rinse water.

After washing, freeze an Angora sweater for added fluff.

Ring around the collar.
What an irksome mark!
What won't wash out easily
cover up with chalk.

Sneakers on the march —
To make them last longer,
spray with household starch.

Lint will come off more easily
if you brush clothes while damp.

Rub salt on red wine stains, then wash in cold
water.

Tip: Fluff up down — and feather — pillows in a
COOL dryer.

Query: *How do you get down from an elephant?*
Ans: You don't, you get down from a duck.

Up The Walls

Have an old room where the ceiling is cracking
and the plaster is peeling? Consider covering with
gay, inexpensive fabric.
   Looks great, helps hold back the damage, and
gives a unified look. Especially with matching
curtains and bedspreads.
   (Use carpet tacks or a staple gun on
plasterboard.)

When papering walls, put a little food coloring in
the wallpaper paste. That way you'll be sure you
covered all the paper.

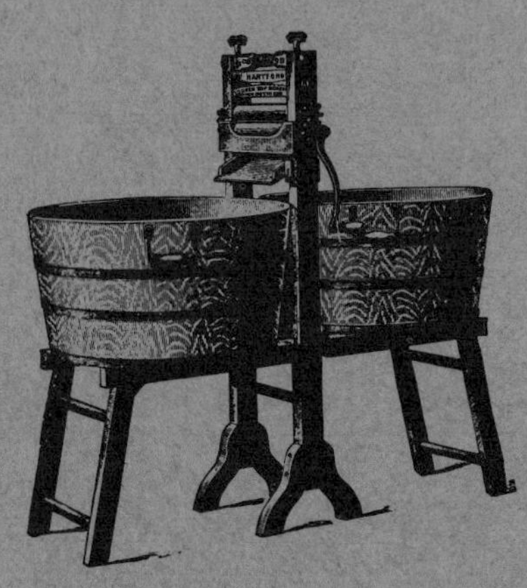

Add a little vinegar to leftover wallpaper paste
and it will keep a long time.

Repair plaster holes without repainting. Add food
coloring the same color as the paint to the plaster.

Fill small holes efficiently with thin Spackle
squirted from an eye dropper.

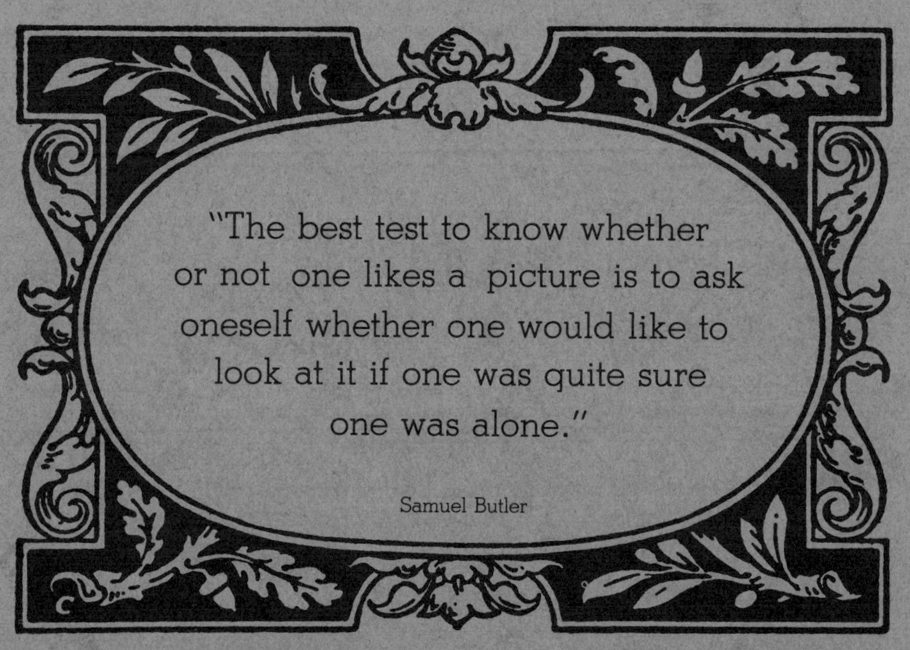

"The best test to know whether
or not one likes a picture is to ask
oneself whether one would like to
look at it if one was quite sure
one was alone."

Samuel Butler

Pet Tips

A ticking alarm clock makes a comforting substitute "mother" for a new puppy or kitten.

A strip of reflecting safety tape on your outdoor pet's collar will make him more easily seen by motorists.

An invisible hairnet on the top of the fishbowl will keep the fish from leaping out.

"Shoot" your cat or dog with a water pistol when he leaps up on the kitchen counter. Effective and harmless — an ideal disciplinary device.

"To his dog,
every man
is Napoleon."

Aldous Huxley

Reflections on Cleaning Bathrooms

Hair today; hair tomorrow.

Still waters run deep.

Tips: A ball of tulle net makes bathtub rings
disappear like magic.

Get up all the bits of a broken glass
with a wet cotton ball.

Shine bathroom fixtures with a soft cloth
dipped in kerosene.

Wash down ceramic tile with baking soda
and bleach. Remove rust with kerosene.

Use white vinegar on glass shower doors.

Use baking soda to remove mildew from
shower curtains.

You won't have a ring around the tub to clean if you sprinkle cleanser in the dirty bath water after you get out of the tub.

Really HOT tip. Before cleaning bathroom walls, turn the shower on HOT. The steam will rise and loosen dirt, making your job easier.

"I believe in getting into hot water.
I think it keeps you clean."

G. K. Chesterton

Get a goldfish bowl.

And a radio, so the fish can swim to music.

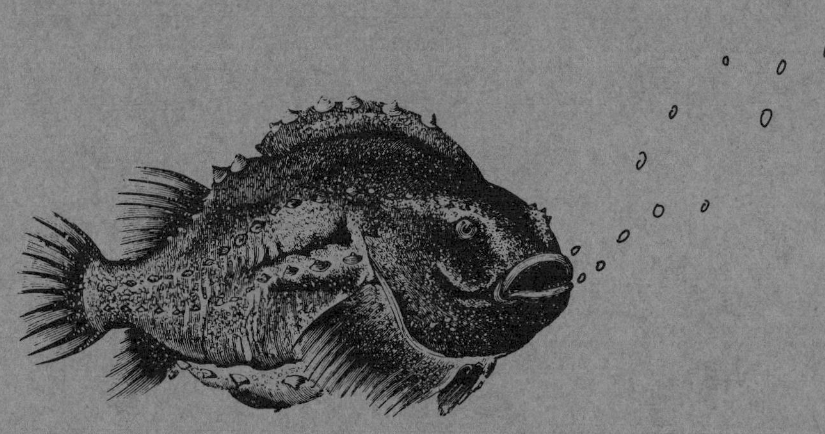

Make Your Bathroom More than a "Necessary Room."

Hang plants above the tub. (Plants thrive on moisture and it's nice to have someone to talk to when you're brushing your teeth.)

Attach a magazine rack so you'll always have something to read.

Paint flowers, stars or clouds on the ceiling.

Make one wall into a family portrait center.

Peeling paint or paper? Bad walls? Cover with *vinyl* wallpaper. Also scrubbable.

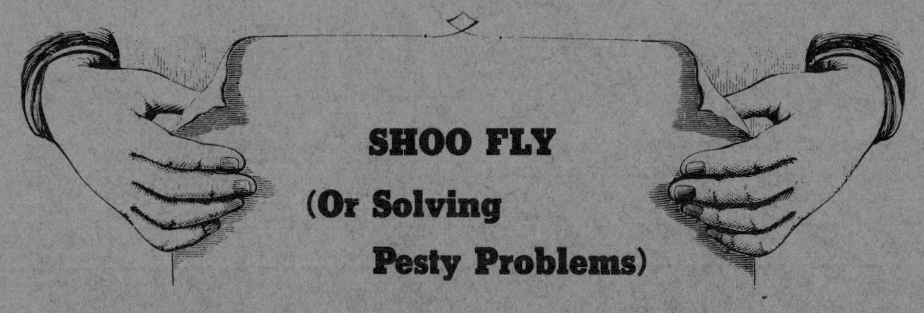

Flies will flee your garbage pail if you sprinkle the bottom with soap flakes after washing and drying in the sun.

A border of marigolds around your garden is a good rabbit deterrent. So is talcum powder.

On the other hand, if you have aphids on your ivy plant, place the pot on an ant hill outdoors. The ants will do the rest.

Ants are deterred by putting cloves in drawer and cabinet corners — and your storage areas smell nice and spicy.

Sprinkled salt and cucumber rinds also turn ants away.

Zap spiders — cobwebs, too — with the suction hose of the vacuum.

Birds after your Blueberries?

Tie fluttery tinfoil ribbons to the top branches.

Or cover with very thin netting.

Or toss an old fur scrap or hat nearby. The birds
will think the hunk of fur is a cat — and scat.

Common "cents"

Rub off the yellow stains caused by dripping tub or sink spouts with a copper penny.

A couple of pennies in the pot makes flowers perkier.

A dime will usually do when you can't find a screwdriver.

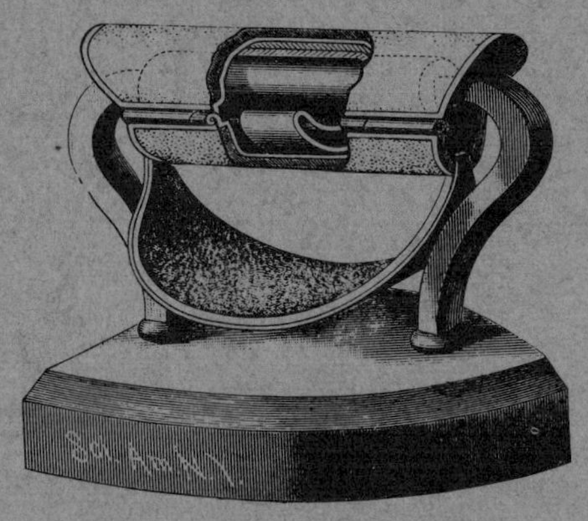

Re: Ironing

Iron embroidery over a turkish towel.

Iron faster over aluminum foil.

Pre-dampen by tossing clothes and a wet towel
into a heatless dryer and let tumble.

For small ironing tasks, keep a heatproof pad in
the kitchen. Iron over the kitchen table or on top
of the counter.

On trips, steam out wrinkles without ironing.
Hang clothes on the shower rod and turn on hot.

(Clothes will wrinkle less if packed in clear plastic
bags.)

Polish off alcohol stains with olive oil. (Rings also respond to lemon juice and the cigarette ashes left over from the party.)

Sprinkle salt on grease stains; rub damp cornstarch on blood stains.

To clean wicker furniture, use spray polish on an old toothbrush.

To clean furniture with intricate carving, dip a very soft toothbrush into liquid polish.

Caring for old furniture is a way of cherishing the past, and preserving a heritage for the future.

On a walnut finish, camouflage shallow scratches by rubbing with the meat of a walnut or Brazil nut.

Light scratches on mahogany can be touched up with iodine. Or shoe polish. Or even children's wax crayons.

Twice a year, give really good furniture a really good wax job.

Spot clean soiled upholstery with art gum.

Treat leather upholstery to a regular polish of 1 part vinegar, 2 parts linseed oil.
Or wipe with a well-beaten egg white.

Use extra slip cover material for arm and back swatches. Saves wear and tear and costly repairs.

Tighten stretched plastic chair seats by dipping a sponge in hot-as-you-can-stand-it water. Squeeze, and put on top of the sag.

Carpet Tactics

In between pickups are quicker with a carpet sweeper.

Use a whisk broom on stairs, carpet edges.

Raise the flattened pile of a thick rug by holding a steam iron *over* the furniture mark.

Always get a cat the same color as your carpet.

Floored Again

Use silver polish to remove crayon marks from linoleum or vinyl.

Use a pencil eraser to remove heel marks.

Get off grease easily by applying ice immediately.

"Nobody said you had to eat off the floor."

Carol Eisen

But, for a change of pace, it's fun to picnic there.

When moving heavy furniture, put old socks on the legs. That way they won't scratch your floors.

Avoid water. It can make boards warp.

But cold tea, used sparingly, is good for floors — and woodwork.

I think that I shall never see
my floors as clean as on TV,
and when the kids' toys start to fall,
I cannot see my floor at all.

Handy Tip — Tie a plastic trash bag to the upright vacuum handle. Declutter as you clean.

Egg on your Floor?
Nothing is slipperier to pick up than spilled raw
egg — unless you cover the mess with salt. Wait a
half hour, and simply sweep up.

The kitchen is to a home what the heart is to the
human body.

Bottled up?
To get the catsup out,
put a *straw* down the spout.
(Then take it out!)

"He who can make a perfect omelet can probably
do nothing else."

Hillaire Belloc

(Nor needs to — as an omelet, green salad, glass
of wine, cheese and fruit dessert make a meal fit
for the fussiest gourmet.)

"I am glad I was not born before tea."

Sydney Smith

Whatever Works Is . . .

The End

About The Author...

Barbara Shook Hazen is a firmly dedicated houseperson — firmly dedicated to the proposition that "Whatever Works Is. . ." which is why she delights in her pet project, teaching the cat to clean the typewriter with her tail.

Originally she hails from Dayton, Ohio, a city well-known for clean living, self-improvement and weed-free lawns. Less originally, she divides her time between New York City (where favorite sports are stamping out soot and avoiding potholes) and Otis, Massachusetts (where her Berkshire cottage boasts of dust balls as big as mice, and vice versa).

She fully lives by her own mottoes, mainly "Never Dust Above Eye Level," and "I'll Be Organized Tomorrow." She sees this book as a Giant Step in the right direction.

About The Designer... ADAIR WILSON

Courtesy of Sue Sims Bender

Editorial direction by Patricia Dreier
Type set in Stymie Light
Printed on Champion Carnival Kraft
Designed by Adair Wilson